On the Irreversibility
of Time

ALSO BY MAME WILLEY

Time Stopped (chapbook)

ON THE IRREVERSIBILITY OF TIME

Poems by Mame Willey

Mame Willey

Antrim House
Simsbury, Connecticut

Library of Congress Control Number: 2011944567

ISBN: 978-1-936482-15-3

First Edition, 2011

Cover painting by Andrea Doughtie
"Flight of Fancy," alkyd on masonite, 16.5" x 20"
www.andreasart.doughtie.com

Photograph of author by Mark Shaw

Book Design by Rennie McQuilkin

Antrim House
860.605-8042
AntrimHouse@comcast.net
www.AntrimHouseBooks.com
21 Goodrich Road, Simsbury, CT 06070

For Joel

ACKNOWLEDGMENTS

Grateful acknowledgment to the following publications where work in this volume first appeared, sometimes in earlier versions:

AGNI (online): "Edward Hopper: Two Poems"
Anthology of New England Writers: "Another Spring"
Bennington College Writing Seminars Alumni Chapbook Series: "Time Stopped," "On The Irreversibility of Time," "Errand," "Visiting My Father in the Hospital," "At Dusk," "The Beautiful Room," "Happiness," "Public Library," "Rain," "Rain II," "Garden Statue," "At Starbucks," "Swimmers," "Passing the Time," "Heading North," "North," "Stopped Short," "You Should Be Here," "Another Spring"
Blueline: "North," "Heading North," "Rain," "Hawks," "I Drove Home From the Movies Without Seeing a Single Car"
California Quarterly: "On the Irreversibility of Time"
Cumberland Poetry Review: "Them"
Entelechy International: "Where I Used to Live"
Hanging Loose: "Group Therapy"
Hunger Mountain: "Garden Statue"
Poetry Motel: "11 P. M."
Slant: "Happiness"
US 1 Worksheets: "Rapid Transit"
White Pelican Review: "Papers"

My thanks to the Bennington College Writing Seminars for giving me an excellent grounding in poetry. I also want to thank the Frost Place Advanced Seminar, in particular the 2010 session with its exceptional group of participants, and faculty members Jeanne Marie Beaumont, Gray Jacobik and Fred Marchant.

And special gratitude to my Howe Library poetry group for feedback and support. Thanks also to Rennie McQuilkin for helping me put together a coherent manuscript.

TABLE OF CONTENTS

III.

IV.

And if you're lost enough to find yourself
By now, pull in your ladder road behind you
And put a sign up CLOSED to all but me.
Then make yourself at home.

Robert Frost, "Directive"

ON THE IRREVERSIBILITY OF TIME

I.

ON THE IRREVERSIBILITY
OF TIME

If I could stretch
my arm as far as it'll go
perhaps I could reach
back to this morning: the last

swallow of coffee,
cold, but delicious
because it is the last
then lacing my boots
suiting up, and
getting out the shovel
the old blue one
with chewed-off corners
that doesn't move the snow
the way it did
five years ago.

Silly to think
I could do this morning
over again.
It might as well be
the middle of April
and this snowfall
not even a memory.
I couldn't get back
to this morning any more
than I could get back
to the Greeks or the Middle Ages
or even to my mother's
final birthday.

SPRING SNOW

on the garage roof
a heap of crystals
shrinking in the sun
water worming its way
into the black
tarpaper then rising
into the blue air
in curls of steam

I guess it's true
nothing is ever lost
but I'm tired of all
this stuff changing
into something else
never really
going away

NORTH

December: everything stops.
Trees put out no leaves
seeds freeze in the ground
dry stalks poke through the snow
till the next storm buries them.

I stand in my doorway on a grey morning
thermometer scarcely an inch above zero
—five degrees, ten—the sun blanked out
by a fog of approaching weather.
In the silence of snow-crusted fields
a jay calls out
as if he were the last one left.

RETIRED, MOVED TO THE COUNTRY

and now a gentleman farmer. Raises a few Black Angus—
Christmas steaks for friends back in Boston. Ten years ago
his place was a working farm. Herd of Holsteins, the kind
you see now mostly on postcards and ice cream cartons and
the prints—black and white cows green hills blue sky—
cranked out for tourists. Dairy farming got to be too damn
hard so the brothers sold the herd and the farm and moved
down to Florida.

The gentleman farmer moved in and divided the big pasture,
half for his cattle, half for his wife's horses. She and her
friends ride through the woods on dirt roads and logging
trails, along old walls now tumbling their stones all over as if
trying to send them back into the ground. At night she and
her husband still dress for dinner the way they did when they
lived in the Back Bay. Bracelets rattle down her arms as she
lifts the bottle of red wine in the renovated dining-room all
polished dark wood.

Yankee across the way, also from Boston, moved up fulltime
years ago after being a summer person since childhood. Got
into local history and now heads the Historical Society and
runs Sunday afternoon summer tours of eighteenth-century
houses and mills and shops, all now the homes of wealthy
flatlanders, mostly summer people. Sometimes he leads
everybody out into the countryside to clamber up hillsides
and look at cellar-holes and abandoned wells and stands of
arthritic apple-trees. When it starts to rain they get back
in their cars and go have tea and cake at the town library
(established 1911) in the new addition, suitable for gallery
space, provided by the will of a recently deceased summer
person.

AT DUSK

We take our mugs of coffee,
Helen her cigarettes
to the back lawn
that slopes into hayfield,
tangled berry-canes,
tumbled stones
and the four birch-trees.

Behind us, in the house,
the girls clean up—
laughter, a boy's name,
thumping music from a radio
turned low so Helen and I
hear only the beats.

Eighty years ago
four girls in long white dresses,
only the dresses visible in the dark
came out of this house to sit
in these same Adirondack chairs.
They placed their cups and saucers
on the broad flat arms
and sipped from thin white china
painted with tiny roses
and set the cups back
with little clicks.

Stars come out, muffled with haze.
No moon. We drink our coffee
from thick blue mugs.
Helen's cigarette
in her unseen hand
floats to her unseen mouth
and back, like a firefly.

If only, back in the house
a girl in a long white dress
sat at the piano,
bare feet sticking
to the worn and sloping floor
and played a waltz by Chopin
too slow for waltzing, and too sad.

AUGUST

It's the hour when
it's dark but the sky's
still lit by blue light
but the birds have all
gone back to the trees.
It's the hour when
three or four stars are
out and a finger-nail
moon sliding down
chasing after the
sun. The hour when
crickets are rasping
in the grass and here
and there fireflies
switch on and off and
moths start hitting the
screens. The hour when
I go through the rooms
closing the windows
lighting a fire
getting out extra blankets.

THEM

Out there in the dark
an owl hooting
something that made
a scraping sound
and a long call
like a horn
I'd never heard before.
Animal or bird?
I hoped bird.

Another call
then another.
I wanted it to stop.
That's when you
on clicking paws
came to lay your head
on the edge of the mattress
asking to be allowed up.

That call again.
Why wouldn't it stop?
Then a chorus of chirps
and yelps not loud enough
to be coyotes
but maybe it was?

You shifted in your sleep
and groaned
or was it a growl?
That's when I
remembered you
were one of them.

HAWKS

When I reached the end of the road they flew over me.
It was a lovely day, if cold. Blue sky, no clouds.
In the fields the shadbush were blooming
early white blossoms that last only a day.
In the woods the leaves were inching out, a green haze.

Over by the brick house and the big rock
the dogs were eating grass, their spring tonic.
When the two hawks flew over, low
shadows bigger than usual with their big fringed wings
I had to remind myself it wasn't me they were after.

UNDERGROUND

You were digging in the sand near a pond
and came up with four dirty yellow tennis balls.
Then all of a sudden you'd gone down
your own hole; I saw the ground
buckle up over your back as you moved.
I called down the hole
but you didn't climb up.
I called again and still nothing.
I'd have to go down after you
underground, my greatest fear.

I made myself wake up then
and I lay there paralyzed for ten minutes.
Was it a portent? Did I have ESP?
After breakfast I called home
but nobody said anything about the dog.

WHERE I USED TO LIVE

Up in the third-floor room with my desk
I was supposed to be writing.
Instead I wasted a lot of time.
Small as it was, my room had four windows.
I'd stand at the one looking down
on the tarpaper roof our neighbor
had built to cover his grapevines.
Once our grey and white tabby
was sunning herself on that roof
on the edge among the grape-leaves.
I saw her yawn, stretch out two splayed paws,
roll over and down right off the roof.
I assume her dignity was injured
but the rest of her was OK.
I watched her walk across the yard
and laid my forearms on the window-frame.
How unhappy I am, I thought,
there's nothing I can do.

URBAN

When we first moved there
just inside the all-important
Cambridge line
but only a block away
from Beacon St., Somerville,
our butcher was on Beacon St.
and next to that the 3-story
apartment building with the plastic
awning over the front stoop
and next to that a shop
that sold live chickens—one
was usually strutting back and forth
behind the window.
In the '60's this seemed
some detail from my mother's past
and sure enough
in a month or two
the shop had closed
the chickens were gone
and the liquor store opened.

SACRAMENTO STREET

It's raining on Sacramento St.
—not hard—somewhere back in those years
where I walk bareheaded, umbrellaless
though the woman coming towards me
is taking no chances—kerchief
around her freshly-done do
umbrella over it all.

It's raining on Sacramento St.
What homesick homeowner, back
at the beginning of the last century
or the end of the one before
finding himself transplanted to a spot
ten minutes' walk from Harvard Yard
gave our street its name?

It's raining on Sacramento St.
Two graduate students on the other side
of the street are having the age-old
argument: will they get wetter
if they run or if they walk?
I know the answer but why bother?
I'm not part of their world.

It's raining on Sacramento St.

RAIN

For two days it tried to rain
and couldn't. Maybe wouldn't.
Sometimes it thundered.
The air held its breath
then rattled the leaves
but it wasn't rain.
At night I sat in bed
reading *Bleak House*
for the fourth time.
The air was still and hot,
moths banged on the screen
and it wouldn't rain.
Then when I'd forgotten, the book
having taken over,
something said *Ah*
and there was the rain, dropping
from leaf to leaf,
rolling down the roof,
making holes in the dust.

PAPERS

September 2002

Yes, I remember the planes hitting the towers
billows of red flame and black smoke
and if I didn't remember TV would remind me
every other week. I remember too the clouds
of dust so thick you couldn't see beyond them
and people on the upper floors
clustered at windows and yes
a man dropping towards the pavement—
I saw that right as it happened, when even TV
was too stunned to censor itself.
But mostly I remember the papers
—TV never bothers with them now—
sailing above the smoke and dust:
letters, memos, files left on the desks of colleagues
like kites, like origami, like paper airplanes.

NOVEMBER 1963

I was making the dessert cake
when the news came over the radio:
The president had been shot.
I tried to call my friend Patricia
but all I got was static.
Later, though, our friends got through
and we told them to go ahead and come for dinner.
The food was all ready.
What else was there to do?

The next night
after a day in front of the TV
we went out for a drink.
No problem getting a baby-sitter—
everyone else was home with the TV.
We went to a bar in Harvard Square
a nice homey one with little tables
and yellowy cream-colored walls.
The kind they don't have anymore.
And no TV.
Not many people there but we saw
a couple we met once at a party.
We hardly knew each other
but we sat and talked for hours.

ON THE RED LINE

we were rattling along at
higher than usual speed
between Harvard and Central
8 A.M. heads bent over phones or books
when the car lifted into the air
four maybe five inches
then dropped back onto the rails.
We all felt it.
We all knew what it meant.
We all looked at each other.

AMHERST, VIRGINIA

After a couple of weeks there
you learned to walk down the back road
past the barns to the railroad bridge
where you'd stand and wait
for the train that went by at 3:36
or thereabouts. When you saw it coming
you waved and waved and the engine
produced two toots, two puffs of black smoke
and slid under the bridge. And you
went on with your walk, thrilled
as any three-year-old at having been recognized.

RAPID TRANSIT

Through the tunnel, black
with a century of soot and oil

in the swaying car
seated between two strangers
eyes on our newspapers
as though forbidden to look up
until the train climbs onto the bridge
into a bright autumn day:

out on the river the sun
lies in a patch of glitter, and
sailboats glide out in twos and threes
as if in conversation.
Blue sky and bluer water, white sails
sun thrown back in our eyes
and then the train slides down
into the other tunnel.

It all goes by too fast for the tug—
regret, nostalgia, whatever.

II.

JUST BEFORE WAKING

I received a letter
the envelope addressed
in an old-fashioned hand
all peaks and angles
like my grandmother's handwriting
on her last letters to family back East
from California where she'd gone
—in vain, it turned out—for her health.
She took along my infant mother.

The letter itself was on thin paper
and written in the same hand.
It would say something important
something that would allow me
at last to make sense of things—

ONLY AT THE OCEAN

where we sat that spring
—bare feet, jeans, heavy sweaters—
around a driftwood fire
drinking wine from paper cups
eating chips and singing protest songs.
Down there, waves pounded onto the sand
and no one went near them.

In summer it was a different ocean.
I was eight. I could swim
then lie on my back
and watch the sky while the waves
lifted me up and slid me down.
When it got dark she made me get out
and put on a sweatshirt
over my damp and sandy suit.
I was shivering and I knew
my lips were purple.

And down below the porch
the tide was going out.
I could almost not hear
tiny waves slapping the sand.
And the salty air, like nothing here
among these unmoving hills
was going dark, and the stars
were coming out, and the moon
like no stars, no moon
anywhere else.

ELDEST CHILD

The water tasted like iron.
There were mosquitoes.
No screens in the windows of our cabins
no glass either. Cold at night
cold in the daytime too
but they made us wear shorts all the time
and we had to swim in the lake every day
except for some of the older girls.

I was exiled to the mountains
while Margie and Anne were at the seashore
with Mother and Daddy.
They could swim in the ocean
go digging for clams with Ruthie
see Shirley Temple on Saturday afternoons.

She'd kicked me out of the family
like I knew she always wanted to.
When I wrote her the first time
the letter back said it was too bad
about the water and the cold
but I'd get used to it.
There wasn't anything
about coming to get me.

ON A DARK SPRING AFTERNOON

I took the dogs to the pond.
They smelled wet for hours.
After the pond we walked up the hill
to where the girls' camp used to be.
There wasn't much left: a tipped-over outhouse
back in the woods, the fallen chimney
of the Infirmary, a wide-open space
where the Main Bungalow had stood.
And near the jumbled stones that were
the foundation of our Senior Bungalow
I yelled myself into a sore throat
when the younger dog, who chases everything
almost got a mouthful of quills
and the porcupine clambered up a tree.

TIME STOPPED

that summer of getting up at six and walking
down through the trees to feed the horses and clean the stalls
then breakfast then rides and lessons maybe a swim
then at six with the horses cooled down
watered and fed and from their stalls
evening sounds of munching and swishing
thumps of hoof on wood and outside
sun spreading low and orange over the treetops
we cleaned the saddles and bridles
you checking to see we did it right
correcting our grammar as we chatted
different from is different from *different than*
the way you corrected the bend of our knees
or ankles when we rode or the angle of our hands

I thought we'd always be doing this I thought so
even when it stopped being light at six
and mornings were so cold I had to get dressed
under the blankets and one day
camp was over and we all went home
on the train to Hartford or Pittsburgh or Baltimore only now
I don't think that way anymore now
that all those horses are gone and most of the counselors
and many of the campers and you are gone who
corrected our grammar and taught us to ride
I went to your service two summers ago
and the camp is gone now really gone and the stable with it
everything torn down or torched for the Fire Department
to practice then bulldozed under

THOUGH NEVER NOTED FOR MY
PHYSICAL GRACE

I am doing a WASP rain dance.
We need rain. The ground's like powder.
The sky's been black for days but no rain

so I'm doing a WASP rain dance:
"Tea for Two" on the same piano, drums, sax
that played for dancing school

—blight of my week—twenty boys and girls
shuffling around the polished floor
while the dried-up many-times-married old lady

in the center of the room
rapped time with her pointer and I kept an eye
on the windows for signs of impending twilight.

How I wished I was one of the boys who didn't wait for dark
and Mother's arrival but snuck into the coatroom
climbed out the window and escaped to Farmington Avenue.

"Tea"—step—"for *Two"*—step—
"and *Two"*—step—"for *Tea"*—step—
though for me it's more like "hop"

because, in those faroff sullen days I made a point
of *not* learning to dance. So today I'm dancing alone
—no one's feet to tromp on—

though the clouds are black and they won't give up a drop.

IN THE PAST

the light was not so strong as what I read
and write by now—bright, white, almost
no shadows. Back then the light was feeble,
yellow. I held my head close to the page
where I sat reading in the living-room—
my father with the paper, Gilbert and Sullivan
on the phonograph, my mother knitting
or fitting together the pieces of the jigsaw
puzzle she kept spread out on the card-table.
Nobody talked or sang along with the music.
Our heads were bent above our reading or
our work, in the yellow light of the past
where shadows collected in corners and hung in doorways,
not like now, where everything is clear and bright.

ERRAND

When I was fifteen you sent me to the hardware store,
the plumbing section, to get you a ball cock
for the toilet that wouldn't stop running.
I guess you were too busy to go yourself
or maybe you were embarrassed, too
though you didn't seem to understand
why I whined and made excuses. I finally went
and the man at the counter smirked or I thought he did
when I spoke the awful words. Later
I explained, making a joke of it, and you
as if now finally getting it, said *"Oh."*

SIXTEEN

While the cocktail party raged on downstairs
I sat at the desk in my bedroom
writing bad poems in a spiral notebook.

Someone came upstairs to use the bathroom
then he came into my room—the door was open—
to chat with me. We knew each other, he was a doctor

like my father. He asked about school and what did I like
to do. I was naïve as they come, but I knew
he was a bit drunk, and only pretending
an interest in my interests.

VISITING MY FATHER IN THE HOSPITAL

He fell on the way from the bathroom—
or was that when he fell out of bed?
Anyway, he was in the hospital
with a cracked trochanter.

You weren't there that day. I was there alone.
He reminisced: "I met your mother at a party.
She was carrying a tray of drinks.
I said to myself, *That's the girl.*"

With my long-ago classical schooling I thought
Hebe, cupbearer to the gods.
With my more recent practical education, undertaken
in hospital basements and church meeting-halls, I thought
even then an Enabler, and even before you met him.

THE BEAUTIFUL ROOM

A big room
on the first floor
lots of light
white walls
white ceiling
two tall windows
fireplace between

but no furniture
just a folding wooden cot
—you were lying on it—
oh, and a Christmas-tree
though it was March now
standing in a corner
dripping yellow needles.

But there were new
blue curtains at the windows
on the floor an Oriental rug
without a single worn spot:
dark blue almost-vines
meshed and locked
and black almost-animals
with long necks like llamas
stood rigid still.

Blankets were pulled
up to your chin.
Your head was raised
on two stacked pillows.
You didn't say a thing.
If it hadn't been a dream
I'd have asked
how's your arthritis
feeling superior
because you have it
and I don't. But it was
a dream and I didn't even
remember your arthritis.

Why this bright room
so unlike your own
dark rooms with crumbling walls
and shabby furniture?
(And that Christmas-tree, too.)
Why no other furniture
not even a chair
for your visiting sister?

PUBLIC LIBRARY

It hadn't changed:
yellow oak cases
high-up dirty windows
brown linoleum
dust mixed with bindery glue—
the smell that says books.

The only new thing
was the computer
that told me my books
were in the stacks.
They hadn't changed either:
metal mesh floor
dark shelves
narrow aisles
room only for one.
I used to wonder
what if I were trapped here
with a sex fiend?
No one was ever there.
No one was there now.

I found my books. They were old
falling out of the covers
pages speckled.
No one had checked them out for years.
When I was young and unhappy
I went to this library
looking for the book
that would change my life.

III.

2:53

The wedge of sunlight on the windowsill
shrinks and disappears. The cat
picks at the screen to get at birds
outside. I yell at her. She stops.
I turn a page. The telephone rings.
I don't answer and it stops. The young dog
lays his head on the old one's rump. He whines.
It's time to go out. The pink geranium
drops a petal on the windowsill.

A blue car drives up the street.
The woman leans out to look at numbers.
On the driveway sparrows and starlings
hop and peck at chunks of bread.
Pigeons glide down to join them.
Behind his fence the rottweiler
rolls his bark around in his throat.
A grey cat trots across the street.
The maple tree unfolds its leaves so slowly
that even if I watched I wouldn't notice
and the depressed man who says he's a psychologist
has started his afternoon walk up to the park and back.

11 P. M.

and quiet as it gets
though a little dog's
yapping, and a jet
flies over my roof
headed northwest—Burlington
Montreal, some city of no
particular romantic reverberation.

The young with their usual disregard
for anyone else's sleep or reading or TV
have gone—the last pickup, radio
set to blank out conversation and even thought
has dropped off its baseball-capped passengers
and the last wired-for-sound car
has throbbed and thudded down the street
shuddering every breastbone on the block.

Now it's time
to sit in bed, lit
by the pyramid of light
the rest of the room
delightfully in shadow
and read my almost-trashy novel
all the brain can take at this hour.
No more cars, the little dog
has gone in, the jet
is already over Vermont.
I can barely hear the teenagers
in the park partying
drinking their illegal beer.

EDWARD HOPPER: TWO POEMS

I think I'm not very human, I didn't want to paint
people posturing and grimacing. What I wanted
to do was to paint sunlight on the side of a house.

— Edward Hopper

I.

There is no dirt:
no oil-stains on the pavement
green in the neon light.
Even the wooden countertop, seen
through the plate-glass window, is clean.

In the movie theatre where the usher
half-asleep, waits with her flashlight,
no one, I think, has stuck chewing-gum
under the seats.

Houses are white, with blue shadows
never dirty, peeling or filmed with salt
from the ocean which is always there
even when you can't see it.
If two people are inside a room
they don't talk or touch, make love
argue or even look at each other.
And if you know that the woman
standing in the doorway, sitting naked in the chair
or leaning on the counter, is the painter's wife,
this is only a fact. It has
nothing to do with her being here
in a world washed clean of distractions.

II. "CHOP SUEY," 1929

Two young women in their plain
daytime dresses and helmet-hats
sit at the window beside
the big red sign outside:
"Chop Suey" in white lights.
At their elbows a square teapot
and empty bowl—like props.

One of these women could be my mother
(the year is right)
that is if she had been so daring
as to sit for a painter
(even one so unconcerned
with matters of the flesh)
so daring as to sit
in a Chinese restaurant
waiting for chop suey.

BROUGHT ALONG ON A BUSINESS VISIT
TO A STRANGER'S HOUSE

They've put me on a sofa in an alcove
—not a room really, just a "space"—
for watching the oversized TV
or reading, though the books
are not inviting: A World Book set
spines unscratched as the day they were bought
Man's Best Friend, Basic Combined Training, Lassie Come Home.
Around the corner another space with the exercise-machines
and a big window holding spring trees
red, yellow, green.

Behind me, windows of another sort—
three oil-paintings done by an amateur hand
seashore scenes in oranges, blues, greens.
A sailboat at anchor, the water made of blue dots
Seurat-style, but the water refuses to lie flat
and threatens to rear right up out of the canvas
just as the wooden steps that lead to the front door
of the cottage tilt at an angle impossible to walk on.
Only with the path along the beach-fence does perspective
lie down and behave as it's supposed to.

They remind me of paintings I used to do myself
back when I still believed practice could overcome
lack of talent. I would not have put mine in these
expensive gilt frames, or hung them in such a conspicuous place.

I see by the signatures they were painted by the lady of the house
who is at the moment down the hall in the computer room
being taught to use a program
for keeping the books of her horse-training business.
She has no idea I'm sitting here writing about her.

GROUP THERAPY

She was thirty-five and quite plain.
Sometimes she strapped a cushion under her waist
to look pregnant. Other times her stomach was flat.
Once after the session I offered her a ride to Cambridge.
She said no thanks and took the subway home.
I never offered again.

One night halfway through she left the session in tears.
Steve went after her. He ran up Comm. Ave.
and brought her back. She was happy.
She was touched that we cared.
Six months later she ran out in tears again.
Steve didn't go after her and neither did anyone else.
We sat there and talked about our own problems.

AT STARBUCKS

I couldn't stop looking at the woman. She'd just come out of
the ladies' room, and she was standing outside the doorway.
Waiting for someone. Tall. Brown hair with a bunch of curls
over her forehead. Makeup but the kind you don't notice.
Fashionably wearing white shirt, black jacket and pants. I
couldn't understand why I needed—yes, *needed*—
to look at her. As if I were sexually attracted to her. Her two
friends came out of the ladies' room and they all got their
coffees and sat at the table just across from ours. She was in
the corner right opposite my chair and I had to deliberately
limit the number of times I looked at her. Then one of the
other women said something and she answered in a baritone
voice. When I looked again her features were already starting
to rearrange themselves.

FRESHMAN COMP

When he still came to class
he wrote about growing up in the North End.
When he was little his friend fell off the pier and drowned.
In high school, a classmate sold drugs.

He stopped coming to class because of a family tragedy:
his cousin in New York was gay and his father shot him.
Did I believe this? "How could you make up
something like that?" K. said when I told her.

He looked desperate but he promised to attend class
and make up the work he'd missed. He was going
        to be a stockbroker.
He smelled—not bad, exactly, only as if
he hadn't changed his underwear for days.

K. said give him another chance—people in charge
always say that though they know
as well as you it's a waste of time.
He came back for maybe a week.
The last time he was half an hour late.

TRISHA

You were in my creative writing class. Pretty and tiny and blonde. You showed me a play you'd written for another class, probably for another school. I don't remember much about it, just that I thought it was pretty good for a college sophomore. I do remember the piece you wrote in class: how when you were in high school you used to drink with your friends in a vacant lot in the neighborhood. You made it sound so civilized: good conversation and all, like a bunch of professors at a cocktail party. But I knew about those teenage gatherings. The yelling. The throwing-up. The smashed bottles. The cops who never show up when the neighbors call in. The last day of class you spoke to me afterwards and I smelled the liquor on your breath. At 10:30 in the morning.

A couple of years later we were on our way in the early morning to the airport with that crazy cabbie who took a "short cut" through parts of Medford I never saw before or since. He stopped to say hi to a friend, a man standing in front of a shuttered liquor store. There was a young woman there, too, small and blonde and bedraggled. The cabbie asked her if she was waiting for the liquor store to open and she said yes. Poor thing, he said to us as he drove on, and I thought, Oh my God.

MR. AND MRS.

When they come home he switches on the radio.
Whatever it is—a singer screaming himself hoarse
meanderings of a saxophone, broodings
of a string quartet—they're better than the thoughts
stuck in his head.

When they come home she likes the silence of an empty house
rooms with no one in them, not even a cat. She wants to watch
her thoughts as they pass through her mind, slowly
or so fast they're just a blur.
She wants to ask, Can't we turn it off?

THUNDER, SOMEWHERE

or perhaps it's a tractor
lugging across a field
a semi rocking the ground
along the river
an airplane hurtling between
city and city too high to see:
a steady grumbling like that of two
bickering all day.

We want it to end in outburst
crash as of furniture thrown
slashes of lightning like cracks in china
rain hurled onto the roof
again and again then slowing
to a steady sobbing
then silence in which the sun emerges
water drips thoughtfully from leaves.

IN THE SUN

You came out of your shop and into the late
summer sun. I was shocked, your face was so pale
as if the sun had bleached it, the way washing
had faded your blue shirt white. Why so pale?
Had you spent all summer under fluorescent tubes
shaping, nailing, gluing the planters
and window-boxes hardly anyone buys
however lovingly made? No, I'm sure
you must have gone out to mow the yard
burn the trash and patch the roof—you've had
the ladder there since June. In another world
where we could put our selves aside, speak freely
I'd have put my hand on your arm and asked, Are you ill?
But in this one, I stood in the sun and said nothing.

STOPPED SHORT

When he finished his coffee
put on his jacket
took the shovel
and went to clear the steps
then the front walk
he was here, the way you
and I are here, he had plans:
poems to send out
reading next month
class to teach tomorrow.
The shoveling done
he'd sit at the computer.
Lines were already
wandering through his head.
He had a wife
and a seven-year-old daughter
who afterwards
would go on with their own plans.

GARDEN STATUE

He's a fat boy with moss-green curls,
empty statue eyes and a sort of simper,
chipped-off feet—wings, too—
if you look behind, where his hands
are bound with ropes of roses.

I say he's a boy but how do I know?
He has tiny breasts like a girl, but another
garland of roses winds round his thigh
concealing what would settle the question.
But I say he's a boy, trussed up with roses

for some ceremony whose purpose is lost
along with the sculptor, as this boy
—if he is a boy—in ten years, twenty,
will also be lost, time and weather
having had their way with him.

PACKAGE TOUR

I caught up on my sleep
at the Tate Gallery
during a slide lecture.
I woke to a view of Llangollen
—the lecturer said "Thlangothlen"—
cows, trees and hills, all
in the red glaze of sunset.
Three days earlier
coming down on the motor-coach
from the ferry and Ireland
—in Dublin we'd been set upon
by shouting twelve-year-old girls
who took my wallet—
we made our only stop in Wales.
But all we saw of Llangollen
was a mall of tea- and souvenir-
shops. We had tea.
On a wall of the public ladies'
teenage girls had written
WE LIVE IN LLANGOLLEN.
THIS PLACE IS A DUMP.

2000

It wasn't just Happy New Year
it was a whole new century
a whole new millennium

though certain pedantic wet-blankets
said it wouldn't really happen
for another year.

They were right but who cared?
The next day we'd date our checks
with a brand-new 2 and 0.

In our tiny town the houses
around the green held open house.
We went to some, mostly to warm up. And eat.

The temperature sank to zero
but we stood outside and watched the footrace
up the hill to the door of the Town House

then walked around rubbing our arms
till the steeple-clock began to bong
and somebody set off a dozen

rather pathetic Roman candles.
(So much for the advertised fireworks.)
Everybody cheered, though, and Jen and I

hugged each other and jumped up and down
because it was a whole new world
and because we were so cold.

HEADING NORTH

The loneliness of little country houses
grey or white no porch no shutters
no ornaments just the one
granite slab at the front door
white flask of bottled gas
on the kitchen side
stacked cylinders
of stovewood on the other
no trees no shrubs the grass
always close-cut
though we never see
anyone pushing the mower.

A car on the two gravelled ruts
next to the stovewood
shirts with hunched shoulders
hanging on the rope in back
between two posts
thread of white smoke from the chimney
but why do we never see
children on the lawn or a dog
the woman taking down the shirts
the man walking out to the field
behind to burn the trash?

IV.

SWIMMERS

She, the object once
of your desire
your confidante as well
but now our weekend host
took us to swim at Duck Pond.
There weren't any ducks, just geese
gulls, and the yellow-jackets
that would send us back to the cabin.

The pond was perfectly round
(some geological quirk, a guidebook told us)
the water warm and see-to-the-bottom clear.
When you and I walked in
a school of minnows flickered past our legs
fish and their shadows on the clean white sand
turning in unison.

WEEKEND

four o'clock Saturday
we will walk to the movies
at the big old theatre
chopped into four tiny ones
done over in Halloween motif
black plastic owls clutching little lamps
swags of black gauze like capes
is it fireproof I wonder

afterwards we will walk across the street
and sit at a formica table
in a room with absolutely no decoration
except for a calendar
and wait for our Chinese takeout
that will leak on the way home
when we take it from the plastic bag
the paper one inside is transparent with oil
we will throw the bamboo shoots and baby corns
to the dog

now it will be time for the news
a *Seinfeld* we've seen a dozen times already
then we'll go upstairs to read
watch the late news and sleep

only nine hours till the Sunday papers

PASSING THE TIME

You'd gone on your trip and I was alone.
But it was time to eat lunch
walk the dog and nap away
last night's insomnia.
Then I had to pick up the car
and by the time I got back
I'd almost forgotten you.
It was nice to sit on the couch
with book and notebook
and practice the dreamy shifts
from reading to writing
then just lie there listening
to some large bird I couldn't see
call out over and over
the same single note.

YOU

were lying on the table, on your back
your skin a dusky purple as of someone
strangled to death. A plastic tube was jammed
into your mouth. Why hadn't they taken it out?

I sat there maybe ten minutes then I thought
I can't stay here all night.
Nothing is going to happen. I got up to go.
I wanted to kiss you but how could I
with that tube in your mouth? So I kissed your forehead.
The place my lips had touched turned dead white
then the purple rushed back in.

I went out to the waiting-room
where I sat with a Flight Nurse
—the copter grounded by fog—who talked of her job
for half an hour till the taxi came
—in the country taxis are scarce at 2 A.M.—
to take me over the highway, across the river
and up the hill to home.

II.

The following morning
I woke at six
after three hours of sleep.
There was fog
the sun shone
as if through grey gauze
a mourning dove was calling
the air was damp
it would be a hot day.

In the next room
your bed was empty
sheets half pulled away.
My eyes ears brain
had taken in what happened
but to my body
you were still there:
we'd get up and eat breakfast
walk the dog, go to our desks.

It would be another week
before it caught up.

RAIN II

Light rain was falling as they started out. If the sun came out
it went right back in again. They walked the three blocks to
the church without talking, the two men under their black
umbrellas and Mary walking ahead bare-headed, refusing to
share the shelter of an umbrella with either Paul or Martin.
Martin asked if she wasn't going to ruin her hair and Mary
only shrugged. She's like that Paul thought, she never
worries about her hair and sometimes it looks it.

They were going to Brad's funeral, that's why nobody was
talking. If you'd asked any one of them four days ago, before
the unexpected and fatal heart attack, all three would have
said they couldn't stand Brad—arrogant and intrusive and
dammit he never shut up. Now they were afraid to say this,
though Paul was prepared to observe, cautiously, Well, he
was a difficult guy— And in the privacy of their bedroom
Mary had told Paul that she was relieved for Adele—she
wouldn't have to put up with Brad anymore.

They slowed down as they turned the corner and saw St.
Stephen's up ahead. Here it is, Martin said, and Mary and
Paul said mm-hm. It was raining harder, and Mary almost
ran up the steps ahead of them because now her hair really
was getting wet. Under the shelter of the Gothic-arched
doorway Paul handed her his handkerchief and she patted
the moisture off her hair and wiped away the long streak of
water beside her nose that looked to Paul like a tear.

SOCIAL

Six people, all of whom
had known each other for years
without really knowing each other
sat in front of the fire
drinking wine before dinner

so I didn't cry
though I wanted to.
I thought
I am the only one here
who is feeling anything.
I am the only one here
with a profound and complex
inner life: the way I used to think
when I was sixteen
or even twenty-six.

In the forced intimacy
of dinner—old china
candles, white tablecloth
talk of dogs and real estate—
I was now grown up
and bored, but not letting on
(I think) and for the moment
I had forgotten you.

I DROVE HOME FROM THE MOVIES
WITHOUT SEEING A SINGLE CAR

No one behind me, and no one coming towards me.
It was just getting dark, the gloomy dark that comes
after an overcast day. That was why
I felt so alone, so abandoned, with no one else
on the road. Or maybe my mind was still back
in the theatre with oversized imaginary people
and it wanted company. But at six o'clock
everyone was indoors eating supper. I imagined
candles, wine bottles, friends in for a meal
while I was still heading home, the only car on the road.

YOU SHOULD BE HERE

I'm sorry you're not here
for this rainy afternoon
to sit in this chair and read or on the bed
here on the top floor up among the leaves.

A rainy afternoon is a good yes a blessed thing
after so many clear and sunny days—
dust in the yard and leaves going limp in the heat.
You should be here now

that the sunny days have gone grey and the rain is falling
running in the gutters milky with pollen.
I wish you could see young people in shorts and T-shirts
    and sandals
walking about bareheaded as if nothing were happening

though if they step in the gutters they'll get their feet wet.
I wish you could see this, read this book and drink this tea
—or coffee—whatever you wish.
You should be here for this rainy afternoon.

ON A DAY WHEN THE DEAD
WERE WALKING

(though, given the circumstances
they were really sitting down)

there in the waiting-room I saw one
reading a magazine and laughing.
Glasses, snow-white mustache
full head of curly white hair
just like the man I saw that time in the subway
sitting opposite, and for five uncomfortable
minutes I thought it might be D.
Nor was it D now, sitting there:
Too short. Too plump. Too cheerful.

It was cold in the lab where the phlebotomist
drew three vials of blood from my arm.
"We keep it cold in here," she said.
"We're always running around,"

then she sent me back to the warm waiting-room
where I saw you, hunched over, not moving
till the nurse called your name.
Your face before had been red but now
it was as white as your beard.
You stared down at the floor, the way you did
on our last drives together, when you sat huddled
in the passenger-seat, with the spring landscape
rolling past and you paid it no mind.

But again, it wasn't you—too tall, too thin
the beard too trim. So I sat there waiting
for my infusion, and passed the time
writing in my notebook
on this day when the dead were walking.

YOU AND ME

We are sitting in the upstairs room
where the windows are open and the breeze comes in
scattering the heat of the day. We sit either end
of the sofa that faces the window that frames
the mountain, each of us with a book. In the field
below the house crows in a tree are scrapping
yacking back and forth and a hawk flies over
high up, with its grating cry.

No, I am sitting in the upstairs room
where the sofa is littered with books and papers, and more
spread out on the floor. Such hectic activity
—so I believe—helps me forget you are not
sitting there on the sofa. Now, the crows and the hawk are gone
and I hear the four notes of the mourning dove.

ANTI-ROMANTIC

I think of you now not so much as before
now that you are tamed by time and distance though
romanticized by same, each remembered instance however trivial
bathed in mystical light and endowed with a weight of significance
which in the rush of everyday it never had.

HAPPINESS

is not continuous.
There is no state of bliss.
You're thinking of something else
and it comes in a little drop:

not sunset over Rome
Mount Olympus transparent
in the blue, sea boiling around rocks
at Land's End. But let's say

you're sitting reading
in your same old chair
in your same old room
seeing what you always see:

rooftops, sparrows on chimneys
bare branches
no clouds, blue sky
and all of a sudden you're happy.

You think, my back's not sore
I'm not mad at anybody
I'm not sad
I'm not going to die
and you settle into the moment
the way you settle into
your same old chair.

I DREAMED I WAS WALKING

down a dirt road in early spring.
It had rained, but it wasn't raining now.
The air smelled like clean laundry.
Little bowls in the road held circles of sky.
Trees accompanied the road on either side—
new leaves like dots, red, yellow, green—
a paler, possibly happier
version of autumn.

Black clouds covered the sky behind me.
It would rain again. But ahead of me
the sky was blue. A watery sun
came out, with no warmth.
Then it was dark again.

I was walking towards a town I knew
only from photographs: white houses
with grey or green roofs, white church
all the whiter for there being no sun
and a single red brick house
up on a knoll behind a white rail fence.

ANOTHER SPRING

She will go into the room
and stand at the window.
Out there another spring
unpacks its fistfuls of leaves
strews yellow pollen
on black pavement
and pulls out purple cones
from the lilac-bush.

At twilight
their odor reaches her
the air is soaked with it.
It says, I am the voice
of all your springs
going back and back and back
and forward, too.

ABOUT THE AUTHOR

Mame Willey grew up in Hartford, Connecticut, and graduated from Vassar College. She then moved to the Boston area, where she married and raised two children, Peter and Katie. She has taught English at Bentley College, Wellesley College, and the University of Massachusetts at Boston. She received an MA in English from the University of Massachusetts at Boston, and an MFA in poetry from the Bennington College Writing Seminars. Now living in Vermont, she teaches in Dartmouth College's Lifelong Education program, ILEAD. Her fiction has appeared in several journals, among them *Hudson Review, Mississippi Review, Hanging Loose,* and *Colorado Quarterly.* Her poetry has been published by journals including *Blueline, California Quarterly, Hunger Mountain, Entelechy International, Slant,* and *Hanging Loose.*

This book is set in Garamond Premier Pro, which had its genesis in 1988 when type-designer Robert Slimbach visited the Plantin-Moretus Museum in Antwerp, Belgium, to study its collection of Claude Garamond's metal punches and typefaces. During the mid-fifteen hundreds, Garamond—a Parisian punch-cutter—produced a refined array of book types that combined an unprecedented degree of balance and elegance, for centuries standing as the pinnacle of beauty and practicality in type-founding. Slimbach has created an entirely new interpretation based on Garamond's designs and on comparable italics cut by Robert Granjon, Garamond's contemporary.

To order additional copies of this book
or other Antrim House titles, contact the publisher at

Antrim House
21 Goodrich Rd., Simsbury, CT 06070
860.217.0023, AntrimHouse@comcast.net
or the house website (www.AntrimHouseBooks.com).

•

On the house website
in addition to information on books
you will find sample poems, upcoming events,
and a "seminar room" featuring supplemental biography,
notes, images, poems, reviews, and
writing suggestions.